TABLE OF CONTENTS

PREFACE 5

Chapter 1 – What Sex Means to God 9

Chapter 2 – What Sex Means to HER 15

Chapter 3 – What Sex Means to HIM 21

Chapter 4 – How to Fulfill HER Physical Sexual Needs 29

Chapter 5 – How to Fulfill HIS Physical Sexual Needs 43

Chapter 6 – What Does Sex Look Like in a Godly Marriage 55

Chapter 7 – Answers to All of Your Other Sex Questions............ 69

FINAL THOUGHTS.. 95

Appendix A – Sex Position Diagrams 99

PREFACE

We would like to start off by saying that we are humbled and honored by the fact that you are reading this book and allowing us to impart Godly, Biblical wisdom into your marriage and into your sex life. We strongly believe that marriage is the most wonderful and spiritually powerful relationship that God has ever created on this earth. When you have a completely fulfilling marriage, which obviously includes the aspect of sexual intimacy, only then will you experience the type of abundant life that God intended for a married couple to have. And to put it bluntly, we believe that sex is one of the most important, foundational building blocks that God has given us to build a healthy marriage upon!

In our marriage ministry, *Graced for Marriage*, we have had many opportunities to educate couples on the various aspects of sex. This includes the emotional side, the physical side and understanding what sex means to both men and women. We have also found that there are many sex-related issues that couples of all ages are facing, but are too uncomfortable to talk about. Instead of sitting idly by while others are struggling year after year, and decade after decade, we have had it impressed upon our hearts to write this simple, yet profound mini-book to help address those sexual issues from a marriage perspective. Our goal is not to be overly graphic or to make you feel uncomfortable, but rest assured that we are not going to avoid using sensitive words or avoid addressing intimate subjects. Whether you have been married for several decades, or are a newlywed, we pray that you will find wisdom and understanding on these pages that will allow you to overcome any sexual issues or questions that may arise in your marriage and ultimately make sex a positive, enjoyable and completely fulfilling aspect of your marriage.

For the current generation, and even for the previous one or two for that matter, sex has been "taken over" and perverted by the world. Yet, the fact of the matter is that sex was created by God to be experienced and enjoyed within the confines of marriage between a man and a woman. In today's Christian culture, the church has almost universally decided to avoid talking about sex with any level of detail. If you do hear anything taught on or preached about sex, it is usually limited to, "God's perfect plan for you is to wait until you are married before having sex." While this is true, we have come to realize that there are practically no Christian resources available that are willing to discuss sex with a level of detail that fully explains many of the unspoken issues that both husbands and wives face on a daily basis.

Our prayer is that by the time you finish this book you will have a greater understanding of sex, both physically and emotionally, and that you will find answers to the questions that you have never discussed before or that have made you too uncomfortable to talk about. We also want you to realize that, with the help of the Holy Spirit, you CAN experience a fulfilling sex life within your marriage, and that His desire and plan is for you to do exactly that!

The Little Red Book On SEX

...For Christian Couples

M. Russell Giveans, PhD

Amber D. Giveans

Copyright © 2019 Giveans

All rights reserved.

ISBN: 978-0-578-56166-0

Unless otherwise indicated, all Scripture quotations are taken from the New King James Version of the Bible.

The Little Red Book on SEX
ISBN: 978-0-578-56166-0
Copyright © 2019 Giveans

Printed in the United States of America. All rights reserved under International Copyright Law. Content may not be reproduced in whole or in part for financial gain without the express written consent of the Authors.

I – What Sex Means to God

Genesis 2:24 – Therefore a man shall leave his father and mother and be joined to his wife, and they shall become one flesh. (NKJV)

That's why a man will leave his own father and mother. He marries a woman, and the two of them become like one person. (NLT)

In the world we live in today, it is often a forgotten fact that God is the one who created sex! It is a beautiful thing that was intended to be solely between a man and woman within the confines of marriage. However, somewhere along the way, Satan and the world have managed to commandeer and pervert sex into what it is today!

If you are someone who sees sex as gross, repulsive, or as the only way to naturally conceive a baby, then we hope that by reading this book you will see the heart behind God's amazing creation, and also realize that sex is an incredibly important factor in the overall health of your marriage!

You see, God created sex to have many powerful purposes within marriage. Obviously, it is the primary way that God established for a woman to conceive a baby with a man, and what a wonderful thing that is! But beyond that, sex serves many other roles between a husband and wife. One such role is that sex is intended to be a unique expression of our love and commitment to each other that only a husband and wife can give. In other words, no matter how much love someone else has for you (i.e. family member, friend, etc.), they will never be able to express that love to you in the deepest, most intimate way possible, which is through sex. When a husband and wife engage in the act of sex, they are a making a physical expression of their oneness to each other, as only they can. In Genesis 2:24, God tells us that when a man and woman make their wedding vows, they are to "leave their father and mother and join with each other, becoming one flesh." This "one flesh" principle is represented by the husband physically entering his wife's body in the most intimate of ways and releasing or implanting part of himself inside of her. And in God's infinite wisdom, He created and intended for this process to be the most physically pleasurable feeling that the human body could ever experience! We also believe that the act of sex (which actually comes in many forms beyond vaginal sex, of which we will discuss in a later chapter) is a wonderful reminder that we are the only ones who fulfill the sexual needs and desires of our spouse, which is a good, holy and enjoyable experience! In fact, this expression of love is so wonderful, and is so incredibly important for the health of your marriage, that we genuinely believe that it is God's intention for husbands and wives to experience sex together on a regular and consistent basis!

In our opinion, which we alluded to earlier, the church has grossly simplified the topic of sex, and given young people (and people of all ages for that matter) the impression that sex is something that should never be discussed, and the details of which should be kept in a vault that only you and your spouse have access to. We feel that this perception has limited good-hearted, God-loving people from having the opportunity to teach and help couples overcome obstacles (whether small or great) when it comes to their sex life. There are a countless number of Christian couples throughout America today that are dealing with issues in their marriage concerning sex, and the vast majority of them have the mindset that they just need to deal with them internally and somehow figure out a way to get by, because after all, no one should know the details of their sex life. If you have been taught this way throughout your life, then it is our prayer that your spiritual eyes will be opened to understand that not only is there nothing wrong with getting Godly advice and counsel when it comes to your sex life, but that it is actually God's desire for you to understand all of the details of sex so that you can make the best decision for dealing with whatever it is that you are facing. And oftentimes, the best decision is to sit down with an experienced couple, who has a heart for marriage, and to allow them to get a brief glimpse into your sex life so that they can give you sound advice on how to overcome whatever it is you are facing. Think about it this way: wouldn't it be better to have a two-hour uncomfortable conversation with someone that you can trust to help you with a sex-related issue as opposed to struggling with the same issue for two decades or longer?

Even though it is our opinion that one of the best ways to overcome any issue that you are facing in your marriage (in addition to turning to God's Word and seeking wisdom from the Holy Spirit) is to sit down with another couple who can guide you through it with Bible-based wisdom. However, we also realize that this can be an extremely challenging conversation to have, especially if you do not have a close relationship with another couple that you can trust. So, with that in mind, God has placed it upon our hearts to write this mini-book. In it we will cover every aspect of sex, and answer (hopefully) every question that could possibly arise within your marriage. This means that we are going to go into great detail about the physical nature of sex, and discuss some very sensitive topics that are quite frankly only discussed in worldly movies, television shows and websites. Instead of allowing the world to be the sole influencer in your sex life, we are accepting the challenge to produce a resource that you will be able to refer to for years or decades to come! Our prayer is that this book will help you find the answers to the many questions that run through the minds of a Christian couple in terms of what you should or shouldn't do, how to do it, and what the many options are that you as a couple have when deciding what your sex life will look like!

II – What Sex Means to HER

Ephesians 5:25 – And to the husbands, you are to demonstrate love for your wives with the same tender devotion that Christ demonstrated to us, his bride. For he died for us, sacrificing himself... (TPT)

While sex should be equally enjoyed by both men and women, what sex actually *means* to each is vastly different! Most people assume that sexual experiences are driven by a desire that both husband and wife have, and thus that desire is acted upon by engaging in sexual activity. However, this sexual desire that typically drives the sex life of a married couple is almost always initiated by the husband. Why is this so? Because for a man, the desire for sex is constantly present and is fueled by the need for a physical release (which we will discuss in the next chapter).

For a woman, however, sex is primarily an emotional experience. There is rarely, if ever, a physical desire within a woman that drives her to initiate a sexual experience. Of course, this varies greatly across women, and you may in fact be a woman who has a higher than normal sex drive, and thus are often the one who initiates sex within your marriage.

But for the majority of women reading this book, there is no sudden, physical urge to have sex, but rather it is a very gradual onset that could take hours, if not days, to peak. If a woman has not been emotionally attended to throughout the day, then she is far less likely to be "in the mood" for sex when the time comes.

Think of it this way: a woman's next sexual experience begins as soon as the prior one has ended. That may sound strange, but let us explain. Once a love-making session is over (from a physical standpoint), what happens next means a great deal to a woman. They want to be communicated to and to have their emotional needs met, since their husband clearly has just had his physical needs met. This doesn't (necessarily) mean she expects a 30-minute, heartfelt conversation on how having sex with her makes you feel, but rather, what do your actions and words communicate to her in that moment? You see, everything you do and say, especially before and after sex, communicates something very deep and meaningful to a woman: the sense of security.

When a man takes the time to acknowledge his wife in between sexual encounters, and to reaffirm their connection through encouraging words and non-sexual physical touch, this makes a woman feel secure in her relationship with him, which speaks volumes about how much he loves her. The opposite of this would be the guy who has sex with his wife, and then sloths over to the couch to watch television, or just goes straight to sleep. These actions also speak volumes to a woman: it says that she is being used as a sex object and there is no emotional connection acknowledged by her husband. This conjures up the exact opposite of feeling secure. These actions open the door to a woman not feeling truly loved and honored but rather just feeling used.

One way for a husband to look at his post-sex actions would be as an investment in his next sexual encounter with his wife. As with all investments, the earlier you make the contribution, the more time it has to grow and increase! When a husband realizes that what he says and does immediately (and the following day) after having sex with his wife plays a large role in his wife's next sexual experience, then his actions should start to line up with his wife's needs and desires.

Speaking of security, think about this truth when it comes to a woman's feelings: nothing makes a woman feel more INSECURE than a selfish, detached man, and nothing makes a woman feel more SECURE than a SELFLESS, SACRIFICIAL man.

This leads us to our last point, which is speaking to your wife's deepest emotional needs.

Throughout our everyday conversations, especially those in which heartfelt topics are being discussed, or where emotions are high, men and women both hear through their deepest needs.

So for women, no matter what the topic or the weight of the conversation (and especially after having sex), she needs to feel and hear encrypted in your spoken words and body language, "After God, you are first place in my life and my number one priority. And no matter how it may seemingly hurt me, I am going to take care of you and put your needs and desires ahead of my own."

If this is the message that your words and actions are speaking to your wife on a daily basis, then your wife will have very little trouble getting "in the mood" for sex, and she will very likely be willing to fulfill your sexual needs/desires when they arise.

Women want to know and feel that they are emotionally connected with their husband before they can even start to think about having sex with him. However, over the past few decades in particular, the church has taught that men and women need to be willing and ready to give their bodies sexually *whenever* their spouse desires it. We simply do not believe this to be true. However, when a husband selflessly does his part and a wife feels secure in his love for her, and she is continually shown that through his words and actions, then she will be more than willing to fulfill her husband's sexual needs. This is the beautiful, God-designed cycle where each spouse's needs are continuously being met! And if you, as husbands, think that it is an impossible task to consistently display your love for your wife through your words and actions, then let us remind you that you can do ALL things through Christ who gives you strength (Philippians 4:13)!

III – What Sex Means to HIM

Song of Solomon 4:6-7 – The sweet, fragrant curves of your body, the soft, spiced contours of your flesh invite me, and I come. I stay until dawn breathes its light and night slips away. You're beautiful from head to toe, my dear love, beautiful beyond compare, absolutely flawless. (The Message)

For a man, sex is by far less complicated than it is for a woman. To quote Mark Gungor (Laugh Your Way to a Better Marriage™), "The only thing a man needs in order to have great sex is for you to show up!" While this may be a very humorous quote, it is essentially the truth!

To a man, sex is very much a physical act that fulfills a deep physical need. That isn't to say that there is no emotional aspect to it, but making an emotional connection is just not the primary motive in a man's heart. What women have to realize is that God made men with a strong sex drive and a desire to be sexually fulfilled on a consistent and regular basis. In fact, a man experiences an erection multiple times each day through no "fault" of his own. And each time this occurs, his mind goes to the area of sex. He may be thinking about his last sexual experience, the hopes of his next sexual experience, or what he can do to get this current urge satisfied. If he has a regular, healthy sex life at home with his wife, then that is exactly where his thoughts will go (and it is our opinion that this is what God intended!). He will start to think about having sex with his wife, maybe envision her naked or anything else that will fulfill this sudden rush of testosterone that has interrupted whatever it was he was doing! And the more he understands his wife (and what we discussed in the prior chapter), the more these sexual urges throughout the day will remind him to fulfill his wife's emotional needs until the time is right for her to fulfill his physical needs. This is what a selfless husband looks like. He takes the opportunity to focus his sexual energy on his wife by doing all of the things that he can do to "invest" in making their next sexual experience that much more fulfilling and rewarding for his wife, not just for himself.

Now, although we said that sex is primarily a physical need for a man (which is very much the case!), there is also a very important emotional need that is met when a man has sex with his wife – one of respect and affirmation.

Like we said in the previous chapter, men and women both hear and perceive through their deepest needs, and for a man, that is having the sense of respect, admiration and affirmation from his wife. However superficial it may seem to a woman, when a man has sex with his wife, it is as if he hears her saying, "I am attracted to you, I desire your body and I am honored to be the one who can fulfill your deepest physical need." A man gets such a boost of confidence with every sexual experience he has with his wife, that without it, he would very likely be living a constantly frustrated and emotionally empty life. This is why regular, consistent sex is so crucial to a man's overall emotional and mental well-being. And, as a side note that needs to be said, regular and consistent sex is the best way to train a man's body to develop the stamina and endurance he needs to maintain an erection during sexual intercourse, which makes the entire experience enjoyable and pleasurable for both him and her. We will discuss this in more detail later, but when a man is forced to go weeks (or longer) between sexual experiences, then it is very likely that he will struggle with sexual dysfunctions (i.e. not being able to maintain his erection, premature ejaculation, etc.). And if you haven't already figured it out, these dysfunctions can absolutely drain a man of his self-worth and his emotional well-being. So, in essence, regular sex not only fulfills the husband's needs, but also allows him to be emotionally and mentally strong enough to fulfill the relational needs of his wife. Sounds like a win-win scenario to us!

One final thought on this subject of what sex means to a man. Although orgasm and ejaculation are the ultimate in sexual fulfillment (and are his primary desires when it comes to sex), this is not the only way that a man's sexual needs can be fulfilled. As we discuss in our book *There's a Grace For That: Following God's Ten Love Commandments for Marriage*, a typical man has what we call "sexual bowls" that need to be filled each and every day. Now, before you wives think, "Do you really expect me to have sex with my husband each and every day?" let us assure you that these bowls are not only filled by sexual intercourse. As a matter of fact, there are many ways that a man's sexual bowls can be filled, and most of them require absolutely no work or effort at all on the part of the wife (hopefully that got your attention!).

Some men have only a few sexual bowls the size of cereal bowls, while others have about a dozen bathtub-sized bowls! Regardless of the magnitude of the sexual need of your husband, it should be very reassuring that you are not required to have sex every day in order to keep your husband fulfilled! Instead, there are several easy ways to fulfill your husband's sexual bowls. These include, but are not limited to:

- A random kiss
- A gentle tap or squeeze of his butt or biceps in passing
- Walking around in your lingerie (where/when appropriate)
- Walking around topless/nude (when/where appropriate)
- Allowing your husband to see you get dressed/undressed
- Allowing your husband to see you get in or get out of the shower
- Allow your husband to give you a "handsy hug" (in which he gets a quick feel of your breasts/butt)
- Mentioning to your husband how excited you are to "be with him" tonight
- Telling your husband about the new lingerie you just bought

Now, you may be wondering how any of these can actually help your husband, and not just get his engines revved up for sex right away. Well, as we stated previously, a man is "turned on" several times every day through spontaneous erections. Further, there are numerous occasions throughout a typical day in which a man is visually reminded about his ever-present sex drive (TV shows, movies, commercials, billboards, inappropriate outfits, etc.). When these biological or environmental stimuli present themselves, a man's reaction is highly correlated to how full his sexual bowls are. Think about this for a minute. If a man is having his sexual bowls filled at home, then he is far less likely to act on his fleshly desires and attempt to fulfill that sudden urge on his own. And when we say "fulfill" here, we do not mean "go out and commit adultery by having sex with another women." Instead, fulfilling this sexual urge for a man can simply be: taking a second look, rewinding that scene to watch it again (literally, or just in his mind), looking up that website, entertaining an inappropriate thought, etc. Now, let us be clear, we are in no way excusing this behavior, or calling it acceptable. But we do want both husbands and wives to know that this is an ongoing, daily struggle that a man deals with as he lives in this fallen world, coupled with a relentless sex drive that was given to men by God. So, in knowing that these are the fleshly temptations that arise when a man is triggered to think about sex (again, numerous time each day), we want to stress the fact that filling a man's sexual bowl at home is absolutely critical to his success in maintaining the purity (of eyes and thoughts) that both of you should desire!

In summary, even though a man is very simple in terms of what sex means to him and how his wife can fulfill his sexual desires, it still takes a willingness and concerted effort on the part of the wife to make this happen. We also realize that there are many variables in life that make this seemingly simple task feel rather daunting, if not impossible, to a woman. If you find yourself in that position, yet you truly want to fulfill the sexual needs of your husband on a regular and consistent basis, then just remember that God has empowered you to do just that, as He is the one who created this desire in your husband in the first place!

IV – How to Fulfill HER Physical Sexual Needs

1 Corinthians 7:3a – The husband should fulfill his wife's sexual needs... (NLT)

Let the husband render to his wife the affection due her... (NKJV)

A husband has the responsibility of meeting the sexual needs of his wife... (TPT)

Now that we have discussed what sex means to both a man and a woman, we are next going to discuss, in explicit detail, the various aspects of physically fulfilling the sexual needs of a woman.

Before we begin, we have two disclaimers:

1) We are going to approach this from the standpoint that the reader has absolutely no previous experience with sex, nor any understanding of the biology and functions of male and female body parts.
2) We are not going to shy away from using technical terms, nor are we going to assume that you "know what we mean," thus, there will be many statements made that exceed the traditional "PG-13" limitations found in most books.

The reason we have decided to do this is because we want this book to be a resource for every single person that reads it, regardless of where they are at in life. We also want to leave no question unanswered (within reason) when it comes to sex and sex-related issues, so that inevitably means there will be uncomfortable topics discussed, depending on your upbringing and perception of sex.

BIOLOGY

The main sexual organ that we are going to discuss in this chapter is a woman's vagina. The vagina is an opening in a woman's body located in the pubic region between her legs through which a man can insert his penis and ejaculate for the purpose of conceiving a baby.

A woman's vagina can vary in terms of the size of the opening, and depending on several factors (both physical and emotional), the muscles inside of this opening can be relaxed or contracted, causing penetration by a penis to range from perfectly comfortable, to very uncomfortable. This also depends on the size of the man's penis as well, so it is important to communicate your feelings during this process of vaginal penetration so that both husband and wife can understand the level of comfort experienced during sexual intercourse.

In addition to what we just discussed, the vagina also contains an amazing little organ called the clitoris (See diagram on Page 32). This is essentially a ball of tissue containing a highly concentrated series of nerve endings. The clitoris is also the most sensitive area on a woman's body (at least when it comes to sexual stimulation), and when directly stimulated, is essentially the primary source of a woman achieving orgasm. Because its location is on the outside of the vagina, just above the opening, it is easy for it to receive direct stimulation. Research also indicates that the clitoral tissue can extend into a woman's vagina, and create a so-called "G-spot" which is located roughly 2-3 inches inside of the vagina along the top wall. This area is obviously most effectively stimulated by a thrusting penis.

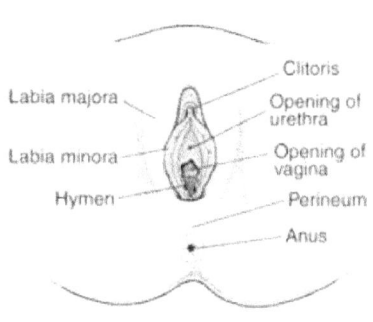

Diagram of a Female Vagina

ORGASM

When enjoying sex as husband and wife, the ultimate goal should be for the wife to successfully achieve an orgasm. Unfortunately, statistics reveal that the majority of women do not experience an orgasm on a regular basis when having sex with their husband. In our opinion, this is primarily due to a lack of knowledge and poor communication.

There are actually several factors (which may vary from woman to woman) that play a role in whether or not a woman will achieve an orgasm. These factors include privacy, mental stress, emotional closeness with her husband, and most importantly, time. When we say "time," we do not mean the time of day (although the majority of women prefer at night, when the house is quiet, the kids are sleeping and the room is mostly dark). What we are referring to is how much time is being spent directly stimulating a woman's body.

We have heard it said that a woman needs anywhere from 5-15 minutes (on average) of direct clitoris stimulation in order to achieve an orgasm. So what does this look like?

Well, the clitoris can be directly stimulated in a variety of ways. The first, and most obvious way, is with her husband's penis. Because the clitoris is located externally on the vagina, stimulating it directly with the penis is sometimes difficult. This is based directly on the wife's anatomy and the husband's anatomy, and how the two fit together.

When the penis is inserted into the vagina, it is often the case that the (external) clitoris is not going to be directly contacted during the thrusting motion. Whether or not the clitoris will be stimulated during thrusting depends on the exact position of the clitoris and the angle of the husband's penis. If thrusting during vaginal sex does not produce an orgasm in your situation, you may want to try a different position (see Appendix A) in which the husband's pelvic area or the base of his penis more directly rubs the clitoris. (We will discuss alternate options for stimulating the wife's clitoris later in this chapter due to the fact that the majority of women do not regularly experience an orgasm through vaginal penetration). Also, remember that for some women there is a G-spot within the vagina, which can, in fact, be stimulated by a thrusting penis inside of the vagina. With any of these scenarios, in which the penis is making directing contact with the clitoris while inserted into the vagina, you must keep in mind that it will most likely take a minimum of 5-15 minutes of direct (pleasurable) contact in order to cause the female to orgasm. The reason we say this is because 5-15 minutes of continual thrusting of an erect penis inside of a vagina is not always possible. For one, this may be uncomfortable for a woman based on the tightness of her vagina, the size of the man's penis, or simply due to the fact that this is somewhat of a traumatic event that the inside of the vagina is experiencing. Second, it is often very difficult for a man to continually thrust for 5-15 minutes without prematurely ejaculating and/or losing his erection. It is certainly not impossible, but it may not be the norm for many men, and so alternative methods of clitoral stimulation will need to be utilized.

Instead of using the erect penis to try and stimulate the clitoris while inside of the vagina, an alternate method is to have the husband use his penis to glide over the clitoris on the outside of the vagina. This is done with the wife lying on her back, and the husband thrusting back and forth on top of her, controlling the amount of pressure applied through the use of his bodyweight (see Appendix A – Diagram 1). The key here is to maintain the proper amount of pressure and lubrication (i.e. body fluid, gel, etc.) so as not to rub the clitoris raw, so to speak.

When a woman is sexually excited, especially through clitoral stimulation, her body naturally secretes a mucous-like substance that keeps her entire vagina lubricated. This can often be used as natural lubrication in this technique of thrusting an erect penis over the clitoris on the outside of the vagina, but if this is not the case for you, then we recommend using additional lubrication to keep the wife comfortable.

This is also a great technique to use when vaginal penetration is painful or uncomfortable for the woman (of which millions of American women are facing). You can stimulate the wife with an erect penis for as long as it takes her to achieve an orgasm. Once the husband feels the urge that ejaculation is imminent, he can either insert the penis into the vagina at the last moment, or he can continue to thrust on the outside of the vagina and simply ejaculate onto his wife's lower stomach.

In addition to using the husband's penis to directly stimulate the clitoris, it is perfectly normal to use other forms of manual stimulation. This can be done with the husband's tongue (oral sex), his hand/finger (hand sex), a sex toy or simply the huband's leg/thigh (rubbing between his wife's legs).

Oral Sex

When it comes to oral sex, this is a topic that is often shied away from, or simply not discussed from a Christian perspective. Many men and women find this very uncomfortable or unsanitary, while others find it wonderfully pleasurable and perfectly acceptable.

Both the giving and receiving of oral sex are very stimulating activities, and can be equally enjoyed by both husband and wife. But before we go into the details, we first want to say two things:

1) From a Christian perspective, there is absolutely nothing wrong with oral sex within a marriage, AS LONG AS both husband and wife are perfectly comfortable with it. If either person does not enjoy it (giving or receiving), then oral sex should simply be eliminated from your sex life.

2) NEVER should either spouse force the other to give or receive oral sex. You should openly discuss your feelings about it, and take the *selfless* stance that if your spouse is not comfortable with it, then it will never be performed within your marriage.

So back to oral sex techniques (if that is something the two of you decide you are comfortable with). In order to directly stimulate the wife's clitoris with the husband's tongue, he will obviously have to have his face in between his wife's legs, close enough for his mouth to be very near the vagina. The advantage here is that his natural saliva can continually be used as lubrication to keep the clitoris moist and comfortable while directly rubbing the clitoris with his tongue. The wife may want to use her own hands to pull back or tighten the skin around the clitoris to more openly expose it, or comfortably position it for direct stimulation. The technique used for oral sex should be clearly communicated until both husband and wife are on the same page as to what feels good. The speed and pressure, as always, are critical to achieving maximum satisfaction. As orgasm is achieved (which may take anywhere from 5 – 15 minutes), the wife will have to let her husband know when to pause, as the clitoris becomes extremely sensitive after an orgasm. Yet, unlike her husband, the wife's body can reset after a very short pause (sometimes within seconds), and oral sex can resume. It should also be noted that a female can experience multiple orgasms in a relatively short amount of time (if communicated and performed correctly), unlike her husband. Again, just do what feels right and remember to communicate if anything needs to be changed or adjusted (see Appendix A – Diagram 5).

Hand Sex

Very similar to oral sex, a "hand job" or "petting" is simply the act of bringing your spouse to orgasm through the use of your hand or fingers (we will use the more dignified term "hand sex" for the purpose of this book). The details are almost exactly the same as what we described in the oral sex section, with the obvious difference of there being no usage of the mouth or tongue.

For a woman to receive hand sex, the same process is involved as with oral sex, except again the husband is using his hand or fingers instead of his mouth and tongue. When the husband directly stimulates his wife's clitoris using his hand or fingers, it is very important that plenty of lubrication is used. As the wife is being turned on, her vagina will naturally secrete a mucous solution, and this can certainly be used as the lubrication if enough is naturally available. If this does not work well in your situation, then we recommend the husband using a lubricant of some kind. The wife should make it very clear as to whether or not there is enough lubrication for the process to be comfortable. She should also be very clear in her communication about whether there is too much or too little pressure, and if the action is too fast or too slow.

As a matter of fact, communication is key during ANY form of sex! You must be open and honest in terms of what you like and don't like, and the amount of pressure and speed that works best for your body.

When it comes to sex toys, the same thing holds true as to what we just mentioned. If both of you are completely comfortable with it, then using some form of a vibrating toy to more intensely stimulate the wife's clitoris is an option. We would encourage you, though, to incorporate the husband's body in some way (penis, hand or tongue) once the wife gets to the point where she is having orgasmic experiences with the vibrating toy. This will enhance the physical connection between the two of you, and not put the emotional/physical connection solely on the function of the sex toy.

One final word on female orgasms: recent statistics show that a relatively small percentage of women experience regular orgasms (to the point where they are satisfied with the frequency in which they occur). If you find yourself as part of this group, then our prayer is that you have found wisdom and hope in this chapter! And on a very personal note, we want you to be encouraged by knowing that by applying the principles we have spelled out in this book, we *both* regularly and consistently experience orgasms nearly every single time that we are together sexually. This is not because we are amazingly gifted in the bedroom! Instead, this is because we both have come to understand each other's body, and we take the time to selflessly fulfill each other completely before we end our session together. We only say this to let you know that it is, in fact, possible for both husband and wife to enjoy sex and experience an orgasm each and every time, and not just wonder when the next one will occur!

In summary, there are clearly several ways to bring a woman to orgasm, and once you determine which way works best for the two of you, then it should be done with regularity and enjoyed by both husband and wife! There is an amazing physiological, emotional and spiritual connection that takes place when a couple experiences orgasmically fulfilling sex together, and that is exactly what God had in mind when He designed it!

V – How to Fulfill HIS Physical Sexual Needs

1 Corinthians 7:3b – ...and the wife should fulfill her husband's sexual needs... (NLT)

...and likewise also the wife render to her husband the affection due him. (NKJV – implied meaning added)

...and likewise, the wife has the responsibility of meeting the sexual needs of her husband. (TPT – implied meaning added)

As we mentioned before, sex for a man is primarily a physical need that is easily satisfied. We have already briefly touched on the secondary emotional benefits of sex for a man, so this chapter is going to be all about the physical components of sex and how to fulfill the strong, natural need for release that a man experiences.

First off, let's discuss the process of a man being "turned on" or otherwise known as experiencing an erection. In simple terms, an erection occurs when the nerves in a man's brain send a message to the blood vessels in the penis to relax the arteries and contract the veins. What this does is allow a higher amount of blood to flow into the penis through the arteries, which then becomes trapped by the closed off veins. When this happens, the penis increases in length and becomes somewhat rigid (hard), producing an erect penis (i.e. erection). Depending on the biology of the man, a flaccid (soft, pre-erection) penis can increase anywhere from 1" - 2" in length, all the way to more than double the length when fully erect.

The pressure that builds up in a man's penis during an erection is a very powerful force psychologically, and nearly all of his attention is focused on this until the erection subsides or is released. A typical erection can last anywhere from 30 seconds to 1 hour (with rare occasions lasting even longer). An erection ends when either the chemical signals naturally subside and the veins are allowed to open up, thus releasing the blood flow back into the body, or the pressure is released following ejaculation.

Again in simple terms, ejaculation occurs when a man's penis is continually aroused physically (although this can spontaneously occur without the penis being touched) and seminal fluid (semen) is ultimately released. When this sexual arousal or stimulation reaches a certain point, a signal is sent to the muscles at the base of the penis which causes them to quickly contract (male orgasm), forcing this seminal fluid (milky white substance) out of the penis. This typically happens through a series of 3-8 waves, each about 1 second apart. This release of semen through the penis (ejaculation) is an incredibly powerful experience, both physically and psychologically, and is/can be a very addictive experience. We should also note that it is biologically possible to ejaculate without this associated orgasm, or even orgasm without ejaculation (but these are not common occurrences).

Finally, after a man orgasms and ejaculates, his erection immediately subsides (at least partially), and the body goes into a "refractory period." This is a period of time in which his body is unable to be sexually aroused and an erection is impossible to attain. The amount of time varies greatly from man to man, but it can be as little as 15 minutes to as many as 15 hours or more (often correlated with age).

So, what causes a man to have an erection? Technically, that is a very complicated answer, but for our purposes, we will simplify it quite a bit. First off, the body naturally and spontaneously experiences an erection several times throughout the day, including at least once at night and then usually again at the end of a man's sleep cycle (early in the morning). These often subside rather quickly, unless of course they are acted upon (either through touch, sight or thoughts). In the context of marriage, some good advice that we have heard is that these random erections should serve as a great reminder for the husband to think about ways he can honor and show love to his wife (since he is more than likely thinking thoughts of how he would like her to "love and honor" him!).

The other way an erection occurs in a man is through physical stimuli. This can be mental (thoughts), visual or physical touch. When a man thinks about or sees almost anything sexual in nature (nudity, seductive outfits, any form of sex being portrayed, etc.) he will commonly experience an erection. This can obviously be used to his advantage (when preparing for sex with his wife), or to his disadvantage (an opportunity to entertain inappropriate thoughts or actions). This is why we so often stress to couples the importance of the wife allowing her husband to see her naked and to let her husband occasionally (and gently) touch her. These brief encounters, if done with regularity, will be the first thing that comes to a man's mind when an erection occurs, which can be very healthy emotionally by bringing greater closeness to a husband and wife.

We should also take this opportunity to remind you of the importance of a woman allowing her husband to see her naked prior to sex, and during sex (as opposed to insisting on being covered up). This visual stimulation plays a pivotal role in the man experiencing and maintaining an erection, which is essential to both physically pleasuring his wife, and to ultimately reaching orgasm and ejaculation.

Now that we have discussed the various aspects of a man's erection, and the factors that are associated with it, we will now discuss the various ways for a wife to physically keep her husband aroused and ultimately bring him to orgasm and ejaculation.

As previously mentioned, an erect penis must be continually aroused or physically stimulated in order to reach the point of orgasm and ejaculation. The first, and most obvious way an erect penis is stimulated to the point of ejaculation is when the penis is inserted into the vagina and then subsequently thrusted back and forth while remaining inside. If this motion is maintained long enough, then the man will reach the point of orgasm and ejaculate inside of the vagina. This is what is known as vaginal sex (also affectionately referred to as "baby-making sex"). This type of sex is the ultimate form of physical bonding between a husband and wife, as the two of them can literally never be closer than they are during this act. Aside from being the only natural way to conceive a baby, vaginal sex is one of the strongest desires within a man, for both physical and emotional reasons. The benefits of connecting physically and emotionally are numerous (to both husband and wife), and this form of sex should be regularly incorporated into every coupe's sex life.

   The reason we use the phrase "this form of sex" is because, as we discussed in the previous chapter, there are actually several forms of sex that a husband and wife can engage in, that are perfectly normal and acceptable, yet do not involve the penis being inserted into the vagina.

Oral Sex

As previously discussed, oral sex is simply defined as the stimulation of the penis or vagina to the point of orgasm through the use of the mouth or tongue. In fact, oral sex is one of the most common forms of sex engaged in by a couple as an alternative to vaginal sex.

For a man to receive oral sex, his penis must be in the erect state, or at least close to it. (However, it is sometimes the case that performing oral sex on a man is the act in which causes him to experience the erection, thus it may begin with a flaccid penis.)

If you don't know already, you will come to realize that there are several possible positions for a man to be in to receive oral sex. However, the most common two are standing up and lying down on his back. The act of oral sex is simply performed by taking the erect penis and inserting it into the wife's mouth. While applying a slight amount of pressure, the wife slides her mouth up and down the shaft of the penis, all the while using her tongue and saliva to maintain adequate lubrication. In terms of the wife's hands, they can either be placed on her husband's legs, on the ground/bed for stability (if he is lying down), or wherever is comfortable. (See Appendix A – Diagrams 6 and 7) In addition, one hand can be placed at the base of the penis, or used as an extension of the mouth to stroke the lubricated penis. Knowing the speed and the pressure is important for ensuring the highest level of satisfaction. This motion/action is continuously performed until the husband reaches orgasm and ejaculates. Once ejaculation is imminent, the decision needs to be made as to whether the husband will ejaculate into his wife's mouth, or if she will pull away from his penis at the last second and allow him to ejaculate onto the ground (if standing), onto his own stomach (if lying down), or into a nearby towel (for the sake of cleanliness). We should stress the fact that the end (ejaculation) of oral sex should be discussed beforehand, and whatever is comfortable for the wife should be the method used.

Hand Sex

For a man to receive hand sex, the wife simply coils her hand around the shaft of her husband's erect penis, and strokes it up and down in a continuous motion. The pressure and speed at which this is done should be directed by the husband to ensure maximum pleasure. Lubrication is usually recommended during this process, but with the correct amount of hand pressure, it may not be needed. As with oral sex, hand sex ends with the husband orgasming and ejaculating, which can obviously be a messy situation. Discussing beforehand what the two of you will do when the ejaculation occurs is important. Again, the husband can ejaculate into his wife's hand, onto his stomach (if lying down) or into a towel. One helpful piece of information to know is that while a man is ejaculating (which usually lasts only a few seconds), the head of his penis is extremely sensitive, and could even be painful if touched. So, as the husband is ejaculating, it is recommended that the wife continue to stroke or hold the shaft of the penis without touching the head. (See Appendix A – Diagram 6)

      For a man, receiving hand sex can be a very exciting experience, especially when done in areas outside of the bedroom (kitchen, couch, car, etc.). One exciting place to experience hand sex, for both the husband and wife, is in the shower/bath. Not only is there the natural lubrication of being wet, but you can also use a variety of additional lubrications that are easily washed away when finished. We actually recommend hair conditioner as lubrication in the shower (as it is not soapy), which keeps things frictionless when combined with the moisture from the shower. The best part of this environment is that after the man ejaculates, the clean-up is actually a very simple and effortless process! In fact, if you have the space, bringing a bench or stool into the shower is a great way to have seated, vaginal sex as well.

As a quick bonus option, another way that a man can achieve orgasm and ejaculate without engaging in vaginal sex is by gliding his penis straight up and down along the upper portion of his wife's buttocks. This can be done with his wife lying down on her stomach and the husband straddling on top of her in order to thrust back and forth, or done with the wife standing up and the husband standing behind her. This would obviously end with the husband ejaculating on the lower portion of his wife's back. If using the standing up method, this is easily done in the shower, with the added benefits of using the water (or conditioner) for lubrication and easy clean-up.

In conclusion, there are many ways to fulfill each other's sexual needs. And as we have discussed, there are also ways to have sex other than traditional vaginal sex. There are obviously more ways than the two that we discussed, but we cannot stress enough the fact that before you decide to engage in them, the two of you must both be comfortable with the sexual activity, and be committed to communicating your feelings before, during and after!

VI – What Does Sex Look Like in a Godly Marriage?

1 Corinthians 7:2-4 – It's good for a man to have a wife, and for a woman to have a husband. Sexual drives are strong, but marriage is strong enough to contain them and provide for a balanced and fulfilling sexual life in a world of sexual disorder. The marriage bed must be a place of mutuality—the husband seeking to satisfy his wife, the wife seeking to satisfy her husband. Marriage is not a place to "stand up for your rights." Marriage is a decision to serve the other, whether in bed or out. (The Message)

As we have previously discussed, what a healthy sex life looks like within a Godly marriage will greatly vary from couple to couple. Generally speaking though, sex should and must be a regular and consistent occurrence within your marriage, as we believe that is exactly what God intended for it to be.

Before we go any further, let us take a brief moment to remind and encourage you with this wisdom – there is nothing off limits within your marital sex life as long as these two things hold true:

1) You do not involve another person(s) or an image of another person(s)
2) You are both completely comfortable with what you are doing.

It's that simple. If you both enjoy a particular style or technique when it comes to sex, then go for it! However, if either (or both) of you are uncomfortable with performing something, then it should simply never be done. Culture, the world, therapists or especially your own spouse should NEVER pressure you into doing something sexually that you are uncomfortable with. Never.

The physical, emotional and psychological connection that takes place between a husband and wife is unmatched by any other single act that they can perform together. Once this truth is fully understood by both husband and wife, they will then see each other's needs, wants and desires in a different light, and will have a much easier time deciding to be selfless and making the necessary sacrifices in order to fulfill their spouse's sexual needs.

Depending on your phase of life, engaging in regular, consistent sex can be a challenging task. If you are young newlyweds in your twenties, then making time for sex is probably a relatively easy task. Couple this with the fact that your stamina, strength and sex drive are likely at their highest levels, and fulfilling each other's sexual needs several times a week is certainly to be expected.

If you are beyond this stage and have children (of any age) still living at home, then making time for regular sex is going to a bit more challenging. But let us encourage you through our own experience in having 4 children (all in a span of just over 5 years!), that if you genuinely desire to fulfill your spouse's sexual needs, then making time for sex at least twice per week is absolutely attainable! Yes, it may take planning or scheduling on most days, or waiting until late at night when all the children are asleep, but if you truly want to make it happen, then you will find the time!

A quick word to mothers: we obviously have a complete understanding and appreciation of what motherhood does to you, physically, emotionally and mentally. It is certainly not easy to operate a household on less sleep than you would like, and while exerting the mental and physical energy it takes to raise and care for a child (not to mention multiple children!). Yet, in the midst of this, we want to remind you of the importance of making time to spend with your husband, especially from a sexual standpoint. Even though you may be exhausted from a tiring day of household chores, running after children, going to work (for working mothers), and everything that comes along with being a mother, you run a serious and potentially devastating risk to your husband's well-being, and to your marriage in general, if you put his needs and desires behind that of your children. If your husband perceives that you give all of your time and energy to the children and to the house, and thus you are left with no energy or desire to be with him sexually at the end of the day, then he is going to slowly distance himself from you and possibly even resent the children's elevated status in your home.

You see, we believe that the single greatest gift you can ever give your children is a father and mother who love each other, serve each other, and make it clear that their roles as husband and wife come before the role of being a parent. If your children can see this from birth through their teenage years, they will develop a healthy perception of marriage, and a deeper respect for the two of you as mom and dad.

A quick word to fathers: we understand the sacrifice that you make as a father, and the long, sometimes exhausting hours you put in away from the home in order to provide as best as you can. We also realize that your natural desire is to simply relax and decompress upon returning home each day. However, this is not a recipe for creating your ideal marriage. Instead, what your wife needs is for you to be present (emotionally and physically) when you return home. She wants you to help around the house, spend time with the children, and most importantly connect with her on an emotional level.

Remember, your wife's sexual experience begins hours before you are actually alone together behind closed doors. In order for her to even think about being in the mood for sex, she needs to see you putting forth the effort to meet her emotional needs, speaking her love language, and carrying your weight with household chores and with the children. Further, you must take the selfless standpoint that your wife needs time to rest (physically and mentally) from her 24/7 job as mom. You can help this tremendously by sacrificially taking the children off her hands for an hour, doing small chores around the house as you see them (before being asked!), and just giving your wife the opportunity to rest. If instead, you come home with a selfish, "I've worked hard all day and need time for myself" attitude, then you are very likely going to struggle in your attempt at getting your wife to have sex with you!

One more word with regards to making a sacrifice to meet your spouse's sexual needs – there are many differing opinions out there on how sex should be viewed from a Biblical *obligation* to your spouse. We have heard both sides of the argument, and everything in between, but let us share with you what has worked flawlessly for us, and what we feel is God's intention for sex within marriage. Although the Bible does in fact state that we are not to "deprive" (NKJV) or "continue to refuse" (TPT) our bodies from each other (1 Corinthians 7:5), it does not say that we are *never* allowed to say *no*.

We have heard many well-meaning, God-loving counselors, therapists and speakers interpret this as "whenever your spouse wants sex, then you should oblige and give it to them." We strongly believe that this interpretation is too simple and quite frankly, unrealistic.

If your spouse is routinely making the selfish decision to put their own wants and desires above yours (going against Philippians 2:3-4), not connecting with you on an emotional level, and not showing you love, respect, and honor throughout the day, then there is no reason that you should be obligated to give of yourself sexually. Instead, we would encourage you to take this opportunity to express to your spouse that although you would like to fulfill their sexual needs, the fact that they are not treating you in a loving manner, and not taking the time to connect with you on a level that brings about feelings of security and respect, makes you not desire to have sex with them. On the flip side, if your spouse is continually showing you love, cherishing you with their words and actions, and spending the time and effort to connect with you and speak your love language, then yes, we truly believe that it is your role and responsibility to give of yourself in a sexual manner to fulfill your spouse's need.

What it really boils down to is this: if your spouse is truly being selfless in their words, thoughts and actions towards you, and making the sacrificial decisions to love, honor and respect you, then this issue of "should I give them sex whenever they desire it" will NEVER be an issue in your marriage. Instead, your selfless spouse will fully understand when you are too exhausted for sex, are dealing with too much on your plate that particular night, or simply cannot give of yourself sexually every single night. They will not WANT to pressure you into having sex, but rather ask, "What can I do to help you throughout the day in order for us to *be together* (sexually) later on?" When you are married to a selfless spouse like this, it is infinitely easier for you to be selfless and make sure that you are giving of yourself on a regular and consistent basis!

So, as you can see, if you and/or your spouse are continually acting selfishly, constantly wanting to have sexual needs fulfilled regardless of what the other is dealing with on that particular day, then you will ALWAYS struggle with this issue in your marriage. One or both of you will resent the fact that you are not having sex, feel guilty for not wanting to, or simply start to see sex as a chore and an undesirable obligation.

In conclusion, let us remind you once again of a few powerful truths and principles that should be present in your God-centered sex life.

From a physical standpoint, as far as sex is concerned, we believe that anything and everything is permitted within your marriage, as long as both husband and wife are completely comfortable with it, and it does NOT include other people or images of other people!

Communication is definitely the key to your success in the bedroom! This actually plays a variety of roles when it comes to maximizing your sexual fulfillment:

A) Maintaining an open line of communication throughout the day, regarding every aspect of your life, is paramount to how close a woman feels to her husband. If he is open with her and willing to discuss anything from every day, mundane details, to life-altering decisions, then she will feel close enough to him to be willing and excited about having regular and consistent sex with him.

B) Communicating your expectations of sex is also essential to experiencing a fulfilling sex life. The frequency in which you have sex is often one of the biggest disconnects in marriage. Thus, having a discussion about how often each of you expect to be intimate is very important. It may be a challenging conversation to have at first, but it will be very much worth it in the long run!

C) Communicate about the details of your sexual experiences. What are you comfortable with doing? What positions feel the best for you (we will discuss this a little more in the last chapter)? How do you keep things interesting and not boring? Where and how do you like to be touched? What type of foreplay works best for you?

D) Finally, if anything is not working right or is not progressing the way you would like or desire, make sure you communicate those feelings! It is far better to have an awkward or difficult conversation now with your spouse, as opposed to going years or even decades with it being a lingering issue in your sex life!

Speaking of communication, one of the best ways to help you overcome any situation in your marriage is to find a couple that can be "marriage mentors" to you and your spouse. In particular, when there is a sex-related issue that you are struggling to overcome, there is no better way to get over that hurdle (aside from the Word of God and the Holy Spirit) than to sit down and communicate your situation with a trusted, experienced couple. This will allow someone with an outside perspective to guide you through your issue with Godly and practical wisdom. It is amazing to us how so many couples continue to struggle with the same issues month after month and year after year, simply due to the fact that they are too embarrassed or ashamed to talk with someone about anything sexual in nature.

We have found, through several years of marriage mentoring, that once a couple is willing to sit down and discuss their issue, the simple act of verbalizing it starts to break down walls and remove the blinders. More often than not, it just takes a small amount of wisdom and encouragement to get someone over the hump and allow them to break through the issue that was holding them back. So please, if you are dealing with something pertaining to your sex life, regardless of the magnitude of the issue (or how intimate the topic is), please reach out to a trusted couple who can help you and your spouse walk through it. If you don't have anyone like that in your life right now, seek guidance and wisdom from the Holy Spirit to lead you to that couple!

We will end this chapter with a final thought: "Men are by nature emotionally modest, while women are by nature sexually modest."

In simple terms, men naturally protect (or suppress) their emotions and don't often allow themselves to be vulnerable to the point where they are comfortable in freely discussing them. Similarly, women naturally protect their sexuality and are not often comfortable with being naked and initiating sexual activity. Obviously, this is a generality and may even be opposite in your marriage!.

Neither one of these traits is *wrong*, but this difference must be respected and nurtured within the confines of marriage. If you bring this modesty out in public (by talking to friends or family about any aspect of your husband's emotions or your wife's sexuality) or if you belittle or disparage your spouse because of their modesty, you can do great damage to your spouse and your marriage. Until you learn to accept and work with your spouse's modesty, you will continue to struggle with it and constantly try to find ways to convince them that they should be different. Remember that this is how God made them and that your primary role is to love and support them as best as you can!

Whether you are an engaged couple reading about some of these topics for the very first time, or you have been married for decades, our prayer is that you have found wisdom on these pages that will help you better understand sex as a whole, and to better appreciate how sex is viewed by your spouse. And when you come to the realization that sex is really all about having a selfless attitude toward your spouse, you will then start to find yourself desiring it more and more, especially when you see the fruit of your spouse being fulfilled in a way that only you can (and should) do! And, if ever you have negative thoughts about whether or not you can truly be a selfless spouse and fulfill your spouse's sexual needs the way that God intended, remember that "God is working in you, giving you the desire and the power to do what pleases Him" (Philippians 2:13 NLT). And having a great sex life within your marriage pleases God!

VII – Answers to All of Your Other Sex Questions!

Proverbs 4:7 – Wisdom *is* the principal thing; therefore get wisdom. And in all your getting, get understanding. (NKJV)

Getting wisdom is the wisest thing you can do! And whatever else you do, develop good judgment. (NLT)

1) **How Often Should We Have Sex?**

As we alluded to, the goal here should be to fulfill your spouse's sexual desires from a heart position of a selfless spouse. If this is truly both of your hearts, then this question should really never have to be asked. However, until you reach that point, here is the best answer that we have been able to come up with:

- Once a month is definitely not often enough!

- Seven days a week is definitely an unrealistic expectation!

- The average that fulfills both spouses' needs is somewhere in the 2-4 times per week range, depending on your age, stage of life, and the natural sex-drive of both husband and wife.

2) **How can we keep our sex life exciting?**

We love this question! The worst thing you can do to your sex life is allow it to become boring and mundane. This is where the saying "variety is the spice of life" comes into play. If one or both of you always expects or experiences the exact same thing every time you have sex, then at some point that is going to become a problem.

Here is our simple recommendation: try different body positions and physical locations! There are a variety of sexual positions that you can explore with each other, depending on your flexibility, biological body part sizes, fitness level, and overall level of mental comfort. You obviously don't want to endanger yourself or your spouse by getting into unsafe or off-balanced positions, and you want to make sure that the position is physically and mentally comfortable for both of you. Other than the classic "missionary position" (with the wife lying on her back with her legs spread and the husband leaning over her), there are many other safe positions that you can experiment with. Please refer to "Appendix A – Sex Position Diagrams" at the end of this book, which gives you non-graphic (yet specific), physical demonstrations for you to work with. There are obviously many more positions for sex, but the ones we have included are the most common and easily performed.

When it comes to exploring new sexual positions, there is something very important that we would like to share with you. As you try a new position for the first time (or the first few times for that matter), there is a very high chance that it simply will not work. Particularly for the husband, if his body (penis) is being stimulated in a new way, then often times this can cause him to lose his erection or prematurely ejaculate, thus abruptly ending the intimate session. If this is the case for you, please do not be discouraged! For a man, this can be a strong blow to his ego, but this sort of thing should not discourage you from continuing to explore new positions! In fact, even if you are very experienced with sex, if there is ever a situation where (for whatever reason) the husband loses his erection and can no longer perform, then just maintain a positive attitude and make sure that you both encourage each other. If this becomes a common occurrence, then obviously it will need to be addressed.

    Another great way to keep things exciting is to explore options for having sex in places other than the bedroom. The first and most obvious alternative would be in the shower. This can be done with the wife standing up and bending forward, or you can incorporate the use of a stool or bench for seated positions if you have the room to do so. Of course, oral sex or hand sex can also easily be enjoyed in the confines of the shower. And depending on your living situation (children, friends, other relatives, etc.), the sofa or love seat is an option, as is the floor in the living room. Be creative, but respectful of each other's comfort level!

3) What do we do if sex is painful for her/him?

Millions of Americans, in particular (but not limited to) women, experience pain when having vaginal sex. In fact, it is commonly reported that women can experience pain the very first time (or even the first few times) that they have vaginal sex. However, if this is an ongoing issue for you, we want to make it clear that our belief is that God is a healing God, and He says over and over in His Word that we are healed (Isaiah 53:5), were healed (1 Peter 2:24) and that He sent His Word to heal us (Psalm 107:20). If you can truly believe and receive this truth from God's Word, and continually speak to your issue (Mark 11:22-23), then we believe that you will see your healing manifested that was already paid for by the stripes that wounded Jesus!

With that said, sometimes there is a length of time that one experiences before receiving their complete healing. During this time, if sex is in fact painful for you (whether endometriosis or some other medical issue), there are many options that husband and wife can enjoy together that do not involve vaginal sex. Several of these options are explained in detail in chapter 5. The one thing we want to add to this is the fact that experiencing pain during vaginal sex is not a reason to abstain from sexual contact altogether with your spouse. We fully understand the physical and mental challenges of not wanting to engage in sex when you are regularly feeling pain during intercourse. However, if you engage in activities that do not involve vaginal intercourse, then you can still experience sexual fulfillment and not risk neglecting this very important aspect of your marriage.

4) Is there anything to help him last longer during sex?

One of the most common sexual issues (erectile dysfunction) that a man faces is either not being able to get and maintain an erection, or not being able to sustain his erection long enough while thrusting to fully enjoy the sexual experience (i.e. premature ejaculation). The good news is that both of these issues are very much correctable, but in most cases it takes time, energy and effort.

If not being able to achieve or maintain an erection is your issue, then this typically has two root causes: physiological abnormality or outside factors affecting you mentally.

For the physiological problem, there are now many different forms of small pills that a man can take to help force the signal to his penis to allow more blood flow to enter and thus achieve an erection. This signal often lasts for a substantial amount of time, or until the pressure is naturally released through orgasm and ejaculation. Research tells us that this most commonly happens to men who are older in age, but that is certainly not always the case. Regardless of your age though, we believe that having to take medication is not the way that God intended, and that if you will believe and receive it, your body will once again have the ability to achieve and maintain an erection without the help of medication.

The second most common source is simply external factors such as stress. When a man's mind is racing, and constantly thinking about the pressures of life (money, job, children, wife, etc.), then this very often translates to some form of sexual dysfunction. If he can retrain his brain to shut off external factors (which is actually an innate ability of a man), then this will allow him to focus on his wife from a sexual standpoint, and to not allow anything else to enter his mind other than the pleasurable task at hand. If you are struggling with this, we highly recommend that you ask the Holy Spirit to help keep your mind clear so that you can focus on experiencing sexual pleasure with your wife.

Finally, if premature ejaculation is an issue for you, then there are two main pieces of advice we would like to share with you. First, there are a series of "exercises" called Kegel exercises that you can perform. This is a term that is perfectly safe to search online, and the techniques will be clearly described. In essence, it is a series of contracting and relaxing the muscles of the pelvic floor, which directly affect sexual function.

The second piece of advice for helping a man to maintain his erection for a longer duration is for him to regularly and consistently engage in sex with his wife! Like any other groupings of muscles in the body, repetition is the best way to train them to perform the way you want them to perform. If you desire for the muscles in and around the penis to maintain their strength throughout a continual thrusting motion, then you will have to build up these muscles just like you would do with your biceps. If a man only has sex (and in this case we are referring to vaginal sex) once every few weeks, then he will never be able to train his body to maintain his erection for a satisfactory duration.

5) Should we abstain from sex while the wife is menstruating?

The short answer to this is absolutely not! As we have mentioned previously, there are many ways to enjoy each other sexually without having vaginal sex, and these methods should absolutely be utilized during this sensitive time. Now, we should say that there are couples out there that continue having vaginal sex life throughout the wife's period as though nothing were different, but that is extremely rare and must be agreed upon by both husband and wife.

If you decide that every fourth week the husband is going to have to wait 6-8 days before having his next sexual release, then you run the risk of having a very frustrated husband (and now the two of you are going to be living in an altered state of hormone and testosterone imbalance!). Instead, if you can have at least one sexual encounter during that week of menstruation, then the husband should be able to cope with the additional time off and "survive" until the normal pattern of sexual activity continues.

6) What should we do if sexual organs intimidate or gross him/her out?

Depending on how you were raised, and how sheltered you were in terms of talking about sex in your family, we have found it to be very common that one or both spouses are uncomfortable around the genitalia of the opposite sex. This could range from thinking that the sexual organ is *gross*, to being intimidated by not knowing what to do with it, or to not even wanting to touch it or see it. Each of these is an understandable, natural reaction if sex (in particular the sex organs) was not openly discussed while growing up, or if sex was engrained in your head to be something that you should have nothing to do with. If you find yourself in this position, we first want to let you know that you are not alone! Many people have this same reaction or perception, simply due to a lack of knowledge or experience.

In our opinion, once you have made the wonderful covenant of marriage with your spouse, and before God, we believe there is a supernatural transformation that takes place when it comes to how you view your body. Instead of your most intimate body parts being something that you protect and not allow anyone of the opposite sex to see or touch, they now become wonderful instruments for your spouse to fully enjoy as their very own. This paradigm shift can be quite dramatic for many people, and thus we encourage young couples to be very gracious with each other and to practice patience as they learn to develop a new perception about their own bodies and about their spouse's body.

Once you are able to fully embrace this new point of view, you will realize that a man's penis is a wonderfully designed organ that is used not only for reproduction, but also for the sexual fulfillment of both the husband and wife. At the same time, a woman's vagina may seem so foreign to a young man, but once he realizes that this is the physical source of sexual fulfillment for a woman, and he decides that he selflessly wants to bring pleasure to his wife in every way possible, then he will understand the wonderful nature of the vagina and that it can be used to connect with his wife on a very deep level. The more and more you engage in sexual activity (of various kinds) with your spouse, the more comfortable you will be in viewing each other's genitalia as natural parts of the body that can bring wonderful enjoyment to both husband and wife!

7) Is it okay to shave/trim my pubic hair?

This is entirely a personal (or couple) preference, and there is no indication to date that says the practice of trimming or shaving your pubic hair is dangerous or hazardous to your health. In fact, there are many options on manicuring your pubic hair, including clipping, shaving, waxing and laser hair removal (which, if done by a professional, is perfectly safe). What we have found is that couples that regularly enjoy oral sex with each other have a higher tendency to want their spouse to trim or completely shave their pubic hair. This obviously makes oral sex more comfortable and seemingly more sanitary for the person giving the oral sex. And for many couples, the look and feel of a trimmed or shaven pubic area is simply more attractive. On the flip side, many couples enjoy the natural look of pubic hair, and for men, it often gives them a feeling of masculinity.

In terms of the downsides, pubic hair grows in that region for a reason. It helps reduce friction and chaffing between the legs, and keep the area generally cool and dry. There is also the risk of irritation, itching and cuts in a very sensitive area if you choose to trim or shave down there.

The bottom line is that this is a topic that should be discussed by both husband and wife before deciding on what you are going to do. The look and feel of pubic hair (or the lack thereof) are very much personal preferences, and whatever you are both comfortable with is the decision that you should go with!

8) How long after baby can/should we have sex?

This obviously can have substantial variability from pregnancy to pregnancy, but in general, 6 weeks to 3 months is the standard amount of time that it takes a woman's body to get back to feeling normal enough for vaginal intercourse. However, if anything took place at birth that caused the wife's vaginal area to require additional time to heal (surgery, tearing, etc.), then this time could be much longer, possibly extending beyond 6 months.

With that being said, having a baby does not mean that you should abstain from having sexual relations for 6 weeks to 6 months post-birth. As we have stated earlier, that is actually doing the husband, and the overall health of the marriage, a lot more damage than you would imagine. And as we have repeatedly mentioned, there are many ways to enjoy each other sexually outside of traditional vaginal sex. Now at the same time though, a husband needs to realize that his wife has just been through a major experience in the delivering of her baby, and thoughts of pleasing him sexually are simply nowhere near the front of her mind!

What we suggest is that you keep an open dialogue about the subject. We forewarn men that you may actually have to go about 1-2 weeks before experiencing a sexual release with your wife, but that wait is worth it compared to what she has had to go through over the prior 9 months! After about 10 days or so, barring extreme circumstances of course, there should be talk of how and what can be done in order to not neglect the sexual needs of the husband. This can be a very difficult time, by the way, with the extreme sleep deprivation, the physical changes that have just taken place, the wife spending every waking thought about the well-being of her new baby, and the overall adjustment of having a newborn in the house. Please be very cautious about bringing up the topic of sex during this fragile time, but also remember that it is extremely important to the mental, emotional and physical well-being of the husband. If you decide to put sex on the back-burner and not keep it as a priority in your marriage for the first few months after giving birth, then you run the risk of the husband feeling neglected or resentful, which can become a strain on the marriage!

9) Is Masturbation Okay?

Masturbation is defined as giving yourself sexual pleasure by touching (stroking, massaging) your genital area to the point of orgasm. And this applies to both men and women! To keep our answer short and to the point, no, masturbation is not okay. The real question is actually, "why do you feel the need to masturbate?" It is our opinion that if you are being sexually fulfilled by your spouse (which includes communicating with your spouse about the specific sexual needs and desires that you have and how to best have those needs fulfilled), then the easier it is to resist any urge that may arise for you to engage in masturbation. Remember, the typical male has a very strong desire for a sexual release every 72 hours or less (and there are also women who desire a sexual release within a similar time frame), so if the two of you are not having sex at least that often, then you are increasing the likelihood that this desire will become a serious temptation for whichever spouse has the stronger sex drive.

10) What Do We Do if Pornography is an Issue?

Research has shown that pornography can be as addictive, if not more so, than many illicit drugs. We are by no means addiction experts, but the earlier someone is exposed to pornography and the frequency in which it is viewed both play a major role in the level of addiction that is experienced. If you feel that either spouse is truly "addicted" to pornography (meaning they continuously view it, possibly on a daily basis, and they simply cannot stop in their own strength), then you may need to seek the help of someone who is trained in addiction therapy.

In general, sporadic pornography use within marriage is often a symptom of not being sexually fulfilled by one's spouse. When each of you is experiencing satisfying and consistent sex, then the likelihood of being drawn into the fleshy desire to look at pornography is greatly diminished. That isn't to say the desire becomes non-existent, but simply knowing that your spouse is willing and excited about fulfilling your sexual needs can (and should) give you the mental strength to dwell on thoughts of your spouse as opposed to pictures or videos of other people. For men in particular (who are by design very visual beings), having mental images of their wife's body can be a wonderful deterrent to the constant bombardment of sexual imagery in the world today. If he is experiencing regular sex, and having his sexual bowls consistently filled at home (seeing his wife naked, being allowed to gently touch at random times other than just during sex, etc.), then these images and experiences will keep his sex drive at bay until the next time the two of you can be together sexually.

Lastly, another great way to help a man overcome the temptation to look at pornography is by having a trusted accountability partner that he can share his victories and his struggles with. Having someone to be accountable to has many benefits, and is more often than not the catalyst needed to make the change for the better!

11) What is "Sexting" and is it okay for us to do?

Sexting, which is a term coined in the past 15 years with the arrival of smart phones, text messaging and camera phones, is simply the sending and receiving of sexually explicit text messages and/or pictures. It is primarily done by the teenage and 20-something demographic, but it certainly is not entirely limited to those demographics. Our stance is that "extreme caution" should be taken if you decide to engage in this activity with your spouse, as there are so many risks that are involved. How would you feel if you sent a message or picture to the wrong person? This could not only permanently scar an outside relationship, but in some cases it may result in you being fired from your job or even breaking a law! There is also the chance of someone innocently scrolling through your phone (child, friend, etc.) and running across a picture or message that will forever change how they see you (figuratively and literally).

So in general, we advise people to stay away from it entirely, but if you are very careful with what you are doing, and both you and your spouse enjoy it, then there is nothing inherently wrong about it, so by all means "sext" away!

12) What if I have a troubled history with sex?

If either husband or wife has a troubled history when it comes to sex (abuse, unhealthy view, addiction, etc.), then one of the best ways to overcome this and to heal from it is to find someone that you can be open and honest with and freely discuss your issue. Of course the first person you will want to talk to about this is your spouse, and in some cases this can be the perfect recipe for success. And as the spouse, it is going to take an incredible amount of patience, grace, mercy, forgiveness or whatever else the situation calls for in order for true and complete healing to take place.

If it is decided that someone other than your spouse is needed (a trusted same-gender friend, a marriage mentor, a counselor, a therapist, a pastor, etc.), then we highly encourage you to find the mental strength required to lay aside any shame or embarrassment and discuss this issue with someone that you can fully trust to help you through your situation. And of course, as a Christian couple, we always recommend that you first and foremost take this issue to the Lord and trust and allow Him to supernaturally heal any wounds that are present in your life concerning sex.

13) What Does the Bible Say About "Oral Sex?"

Although this topic is rarely (if ever!) talked about from a Biblical standpoint, we want to show you from the Bible what we believe is a very clear use of oral sex in Biblical times.

Song of Solomon 4:12-13,15 (NLT)

Man Speaking:

[12] "You are my private garden, my treasure, my bride, a secluded spring, a hidden fountain.
[13] Your thighs shelter a paradise of pomegranates with rare spices—
[15] You are a garden fountain, a well of fresh water streaming down from Lebanon's mountains.

Song of Solomon 4:16 (NLT)

Woman Speaking:

[16] "Awake, north wind! Rise up, south wind! Blow on my garden and spread its fragrance all around. Come into your garden, my love; taste its finest fruits."

      For the sake of not being ambiguous, we will give you our straightforward interpretation of this. When the young man speaks of his bride as a "private garden, a secluded spring and a hidden fountain" this is clearly in reference to her vagina, of which he "treasures." He even refers to her body's natural lubrication by comparing it to a "secluded spring and a hidden fountain." And if you didn't catch all of that right away, he is very blunt in his next expression of "your thighs shelter a paradise of pomegranates."

After he declares the fact that he treasures her vagina and its role as a source of sexual pleasure, the bride then encourages him to be turned on by getting his mouth (north wind) and penis (south wind) ready for a very stimulating sexual encounter. She ends her comments with the invitation for him to come down to her vagina area (her "fruit garden," which the young man just clearly mentions was "sheltered between her thighs") and "taste of her finest fruits," which is clearly done with the mouth and tongue.

So in our opinion, we see clear Biblical approval that oral sex is perfectly acceptable and even encouraged within a Godly marriage. Again, we want to be clear that if both husband and wife are not completely comfortable with this, then it should be agreed by both that oral sex is not going to be a part of your sex life. But, if both of you are open to oral sex, then there is absolutely nothing wrong with it, and now you can have the assurance that the Bible even approves and encourages it within the confines of marriage.

14) Does Penis Size Matter?

It truly is amazing how this one question has become so popular across America, and the world! There is probably not a week that goes by that every man is not somehow reminded about the size of their penis. And to be quite honest, this can and is a major issue/concern for millions of American men. One of the main culprits to this ridiculous issue is the pornography industry. First of all, pornography gives both men and women an unhealthy perspective on body image, giving the impression that in order to have great sex the woman needs to have a slender body, small waist and large breasts. Obviously, this is simply not true!

Second, nearly all adult male actors have exceptionally large penises, often 8" or longer. Men (and women) who see this get the perception that a large penis is required to have great sex. Again, this is simply not true! While it is true that there are a number of sexual positions that are only able to be performed if the husband has an erect penis that is a certain length, you must also remember that most of these positions are uncomfortable and not pleasurable or realistic! Recent research has shown that roughly 80% of men have an erect penis that is in the 4.5" – 6.5" range. If you are in this range (or larger), then you will have no problem performing the vast majority of sexual positions. If you are on the lower end of this range (or slightly shorter), then you will simply need to modify a few of the positions and/or just use certain positions that work best for you!

In order to truly have great sex, both husband and wife must fully embrace their bodies and learn to use them in the most effective way possible to please their spouse. For a man, this means taking the time to sexually pleasure his wife in whatever method works best for her (direct clitoral stimulation, etc.), and learning to use his penis (regardless of size) to stimulate the right spots and to last long enough to fulfill his wife.

15) What if I have body-image issues?

Millions of Americans have a psychological issue with how their body looks. There may be a multitude of reasons for this, but it usually manifests itself in a similar fashion: you don't like seeing your body naked and you certainly don't want others to see you naked either. As you would imagine, this can cause serious issues within a marriage relationship.

Without claiming to be formally trained in dealing with body-image issues, there are a few things that we would like to share with you.

First, as we have mentioned earlier, men are very visual when it comes to sex. So, if the wife is having body-image issues, and she prevents her husband from seeing her naked both in non-sexual situations and also before and during sex, then this is going to lead to some very negative (and often unintended) consequences within your marriage. The same thing applies if the husband is having body-image issues. When a man has an issue with his body, it will likely lead to him rejecting any compliments from his wife about his physical appearance. This, of course, will have a negative, snowball effect through the husband never hearing positive comments about how his wife is physically attracted to him, thus making his body image issue even worse.

In order to overcome these potentially devastating consequences, it is imperative that each husband and wife learn to accept their body as a beautiful creation of God. You see, one of the most attractive attributes of both men and women is confidence. When you are confident that your body is beautiful, and desirable, then your spouse will see that and sense that, and it will cause them to be more attracted to you physically.

Also, in addition to being confident in your own skin, another very attractive attribute is when your spouse can see you making a concerted effort to take care of your body from a physical standpoint. This includes exercising, eating healthy, dressing nicely or just maintaining your overall appearance. When your spouse sees you making the effort to look and feel your best, then this often speaks volumes to them in terms of how much you care about maintaining a level of physical attractiveness in their eyes. Just because you may not look like you did when you were twenty-one, doesn't mean that you cannot still be as physically and sexually attractive!

In conclusion, you do not have to have a perfect body in order to have a fulfilling sex life. However, you do have to be confident in who you are, and allow your spouse to compliment you, touch you and look at you. If any of these are an issue for you, then we strongly suggest that you find someone that you can talk to about it, and who can help you get to the point of overcoming these issues as it pertains to your physical body!

Final Thoughts

It doesn't matter if you are newlyweds, or have been married for 50+ years, it will always be true that sex plays a vitally important role within your marriage. It is essential to the health of every marriage that both husband and wife be on the same page when it comes to their sex life, whether this is having the right emotional outlook, or simply understanding all of the physical components of sex.

When a husband understands that his wife's emotional needs must be filled throughout the day, and how to best meet those needs, then he will have the pleasure of seeing his wife experience a higher level of sexual fulfillment that will bring them closer together than ever before!

And when a wife understands that her husband's sexual needs must be fulfilled regularly and consistently (at the very least once per week), and that his "sexual bowls" need to be filled on a daily basis, then she will have the pleasure of seeing her husband experience a new, higher level of emotional fulfillment that will bring them closer together than ever before!

Even though we have shared a great deal of information with you, please do not feel overwhelmed! Once you both decide to selflessly serve each other through sex, and you discuss what areas of your sex life need to be improved upon, remember this principle: sex with your spouse should be a fun experience! The more you work on communicating with each other, and fulfilling each other's needs (emotional and physical), then the more you will start to look forward to being intimate with each other!

After reading this book, our prayer is that you now have a better and more complete understanding of all of the aspects of sex that are so crucial to you experiencing a wonderful and successful marriage. We also trust that the Holy Spirit will reinvigorate your sexual passion for each other and bring to your remembrance the wisdom behind the words on these pages. If you will decide to prioritize your sexual relationship with your spouse, and make the selfless decision to fulfill the needs of your spouse, as only you can, we believe that you will find yourselves united together at an emotional, physical and spiritual level that most people never experience. And remember, God designed sex as a wonderful and powerful tool for a husband and wife to use as they build a successful marriage together, as long as you use that tool correctly and wisely!

If you ever have any questions or issues in the area of sex, we would love to hear from you! Please feel free to reach out to us in complete confidence by emailing us at –
info@gracedformarriage.com

Appendix A – Sex Position Diagrams

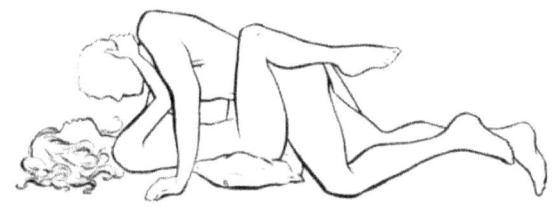

1 - Guy on Top

2 - Girl on Top

3 - Girl on Top Reverse

4 - Kneeling from Behind

5 - Oral Sex on Her (Laying)

6 - Oral Sex on Him (Laying)

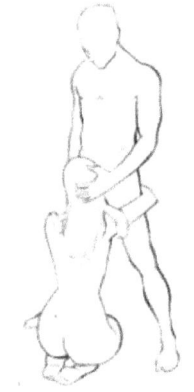

7 - Oral Sex on Him (Standing)   8 - Oral Sex on Her (Sitting)

9 - Seated Reverse   10 - Seated Facing

We are dedicating this book to each other! We first of all thank God for His revelation on this subject, and for allowing both of us to be comfortable sharing this information with other couples. We are also forever grateful to each other for being open and willing to discuss these topics, and to implement the knowledge that we have been given! Without it, our marriage would be a fraction of what it is today!

www.ingramcontent.com/pod-product-compliance
Lightning Source LLC
Chambersburg PA
CBHW071409290426
44108CB00014B/1746